CALIBAN'S ISLAND

A one-act dramedy by
Diana Burbano

www.youthplays.com
info@youthplays.com
424-703-5315

 ISBN 978-1-62088-633-5.

COPYRIGHT RULES TO REMEMBER

1. To produce this play, you must receive prior written permission from YouthPLAYS and pay the required royalty.

2. You must pay a royalty each time the play is performed in the presence of audience members outside of the cast and crew. Royalties are due whether or not admission is charged, whether or not the play is presented for profit, for charity or for educational purposes, or whether or not anyone associated with the production is being paid.

3. No changes, including cuts or additions, are permitted to the script without written prior permission from YouthPLAYS.

4. Do not copy this book or any part of it without written permission from YouthPLAYS.

5. Credit to the author and YouthPLAYS is required on all programs and other promotional items associated with this play's performance.

When you pay royalties, you are recognizing the hard work that went into creating the play and making a statement that a play is something of value. We think this is important, and we hope that everyone will do the right thing, thus allowing playwrights to generate income and continue to create wonderful new works for the stage.

Plays are owned by the playwrights who wrote them. Violating a playwright's copyright is a very serious matter and violates both United States and international copyright law. Infringement is punishable by actual damages and attorneys' fees, statutory damages of up to $150,000 per incident, and even possible criminal sanctions. **Infringement is theft. Don't do it.**

Have a question about copyright? Please contact us by email at info@youthplays.com or by phone at 424-703-5315. When in doubt, please ask.

CAST OF CHARACTERS

MIRA, a young girl. Impulsive, big heart full of love, wants love in return. Powerful witch. Any ethnicity.

CAL, horned half-human, half-monster. A wild thing. Huge heart. Any ethnicity. Male.

FLUFFY, a small fairy. Deceptively cute. Very physical. A fairy Harpo Marx. Speaks in gibberish. Any ethnicity. Male or female.

VI, a girl, about twelve or thirteen. Funny, smart, daring girl, very comfortable dressed as a boy. Twin to Bast. Any ethnicity.

BAST, a boy, about twelve or thirteen. Intellectual, gangly, interested in life. Not terribly interested in sword fighting or mayhem, twin to Vi. Any ethnicity.

NOTE/MAGIC

All illusions should be made with light and sound. Magic to lift someone would be the old Darth Vader trick of actor A squeezing his hand and actor B lifting himself up off the ground.

DEDICATION

For Lionel, who is the most magical creature I know.

PROLOGUE

(Sounds of a shipwreck. A bright light is seen zooming around the stage. [This could be FLUFFY with a flashlight.] We see only flashes of light and hear loud sounds of the crashing of the sea. Screams and then a loud crack. The sound of a struggle then silence. A splash.)

(Blackout.)

SCENE 1

(Lights up on a tropical island, strewn with debris from last night's storm, sunny, calm and beautiful. VI, a young girl, is asleep in the sand, a blanket of seaweed on her, her clothes in tatters.)

(CAL, a creature of myth, horned, with intelligent eyes and the ability to walk upright is singing to himself while rifling through a trunk.)

CAL: *(Song:)* FULL FATHOM FIVE THY BROTHER LIES,
HIS BONNY HEAD IS NOW A STONE.
THE HAPPY THOUGHTS THAT IN HIM LAY
ARE NOW LOST, AND TO YOU GONE.
HE DOES SUFFER A SEA-CHANGE,
INTO SOMETHING WILD AND STRANGE,
SEA-COWS URGE HIM TO REBEL!
HARK! I HEAR THEM, DING DONG BELL!
FULL FATHOM FIVE THY SISTER LAY.
HER FATE ENTWINED WITH ME AND MINE.
THE RAGS SHE WEARS YOU DID MISLAY,
AND NOW SHE WEEPS IN THE MOONSHINE.
SHE MAKES UNTO HER OWN SEA-CHANGE,
INTO SOMETHING PASSING STRANGE,
SHE ALONE MUST RING HER KNELL!
HARK, DO YOU HEAR HER? DING DONG BELL!

(He pulls out dresses, shoes, books, lays them on the sand, trying

on some of the more interesting items.)

(Muttering.) Too small, too big, too grand, ooh book-ses will do. Pocket one or two for me trouble. Hey. *(Sniffs like a dog.)* Ahhh…that's the smell of man. Strange how long it's been.

(Plays on a flute and puts a pair of spectacles on his head. The flute playing arouses the girl from her sleep.)

VI: *(She is dreaming of something frightening. Trying to wake up:)* We're lost, wild water, Bast, hold on to my hand! BAST! Leave the books behind! Bast…BAST! *(Wakes, looks around wildly:)* Bast…oh… *(Sees Cal and the trunk:)* Get away from that, that belongs to my brother!

(Tries to wrench trunk away, gets into a fierce game of tug of war until she gets a good look at Cal.)

Oh!

(Drops trunk. Her hand goes to her belt where a sword should be. Cal merely smiles.)

CAL: Hain't nuthin' gonna fit me no-how. Tough to pull petticoats on over the horns. Don't I look a fine thing in these gees and gaws?

VI: *(Cautiously:)* What…who are you, sir?

CAL: Sir! Psttt, that's a laugh and a half. If'n I knew I was gonna be addressed as sir, I'd 'a washed this month. You can call me Cal, small-ie. Leave the knighthoods and niceties to your kind. And you, I take it you are… *(Looks at side of trunk:)* East India Shipping Company?

VI: Er. No. I'm called Vi. Those are the people who made the trunk.

CAL: Well made, too, lasted tough through the storm.

VI: The storm! What end met the ship?

CAL: In toothpicks. *(Not unkindly:)* You've lost everything. 'cept what's in here.

VI: Oh, twinnie-twinsie.

CAL: Twinsie?

VI: My brother Bast. Those spectacles you are wearing, they belong to him.

CAL: B'longed. B'longs t' me now. Found 'em. Founds you too... Mebbe you b'longs to me now too.

VI: You can't own another human being. *(Considers Cal's odd appearance:)* Are you a human being?

CAL: Half. On me mother's side. 'Course you can own other beings, if'n you have a bent for the tyrannical. Don't fret small-ie, I don't want you tho', you eats too much prob'ly, and cries, all girly like.

VI: Don't care to cry, or be gentle and delicate. My Bast and I used to swap clothes when we were little. I'd run in his togs, and he in mine, and no one could tell which was which. I was always the one to give a clout to the jaw of some cretin who would pick on Bast for being "soft." He wasn't soft! Just smarter, and quieter and far gentler than me...

CAL: What were you tykes doin' roamin' so far from home?

VI: We aren't tykes. We were running away to the Outlands, to make our fortunes. My father, fed up with us and our mixed up ways, said I was to be sent to a finishing school and Bast to join in with the soldiers. Soldiering! He'd never survive! I convinced Bast to escape with me, we have sailed practically since birth, but the storm last night...

CAL: A wicked storm indeed. Almost alive in its fury.

VI: It came upon us quickly. The best I could think to do when we lost all ability to steer was to lash myself to the mast. Bast was trying to salvage his books.

(Cal guiltily and surreptitiously puts books back in the trunk.)

The foolish boy wasn't secure when a wave rolled over us like a herd of wild sea-horses. I grabbed him around the waist and held on as tight as I could, but... One lurch and he was gone. Then, next second, the rope gave, the mast cracked and I was flung into the water. I knew I was done for then, and glad of it. I could join my Bast and my mother. But as I was about to go under, as the water stole my breath, I felt myself lifted into air. I dreamt that a beast, a sea monster had me, but instead of eating me, he dragged me onto a piece of wood and I never sank...oh...it was YOU!

CAL: That's rich. Do I look like a monster to you? *(Scratches his head.)* Never mind, p'raps I do...

VI: You rescued me from the drink!

CAL: Bah, I was fishin' for squid and pulled you into my net's all.

VI: I owe you my life.

CAL: You'll be repayin' the debt soon enough, small-ie. So enjoys yer freedom while you gots it. There's dry togs in here. And this.

(He hands her a sword belt.)

VI: That's the sword my father used at the battle for Dunsinane. It's mine now.

CAL: Yer a right something else, that you are. Yer lucky to be alive, Mister Miss. So stop yer sighin' and buckle on yer sword. Yer gonna need yer wits about you.

(Cal suddenly stops talking. A fairy light appears at his ear. Cal springs up and starts to trot off.)

VI: Where are you going?

CAL: Mab here says she's seen a kidlet, mirror image of ye. Gonna see if he's a breather yet.

VI: Bast!? Did the dolphins save him? Where are you going? Creature…being…SIR?! Wait!

(A few seconds later the spectacles are tossed back. Vi gently polishes them and puts them in her pocket. Starts to run after Cal, but feels guilty about leaving Bast's trunk behind.)

(Vi is about to pick up the trunk when a girl, MIRA, younger than Vi and very pretty, comes into view. A tired and bedraggled Fairy [FLUFFY] is with her. Mira is dressed in wild royal garb and carrying a child's wand with a giant star on the end. Fluffy is also dressed in strange clothes, and pulls at its wings uncomfortably. Should feel vaguely vulgar, like someone trying to tug their undies into place. Fluffy is also frantically balancing a table and some cushions and a tea set.)

MIRA: Please lay out my victuals, kind servant, I faint anon…

(Fluffy clumsily tries to lay out the tea service, but seems unused to using its hands.)

C'mon, you dope-ses, I told you, do it nicely, like in the books, or I won't let you use your magic for ANOTHER day!

FLUFFY: *(Complains dejectedly, in fairy language. [This should be individual to the actor. It should be nonsense sounds that make up the dialogue with freedom to improvise.])*

MIRA: Quickly! I am waiting for Ambassador Berowne of far Navarre!

(Fluffy finds Vi hiding behind the trunk, and makes outrageous signals to Mira.)

And there he is!

VI: Um… I'm not…

MIRA: Stop the chitty-chatty, we have been waiting and waiting! Sit!

(Fluffy hustles Vi into a chair, plops a silly hat on her head and forces a tea cup into her hand. Vi, realizing that she is famished, tries to drink and is dismayed to discover there is no tea. She notices Mira has real tea in hers.)

(Chattering:) It's been an AWFULLY nice stay here in your Duchy, Ambassador dah-ling, but I really must return to the land of Illyria—

VI: You have me mistaken for—

MIRA: HUSH! I'm not done. *(Chomping heartily on a cookie:)* Since you have been thus far lax in granting me the keys to the kingdom, and the rights to all pies and cookies therein, I shall insist—

VI: As long as you are going to keep me trapped here and chat-chat chatting at me, can I at least have a cookie and a cuppa tea? I'm right done in. *(Sneezes.)* And feeling bedraggle-y.

MIRA: *(Astonished:) Tea*? And a…cookie? Really?

VI: Fact is, I'm gonna make myself to home. Ta.

(Vi pours herself a drink and starts to eat greedily.)

MIRA: Holy Macdufflings!

(Fluffy makes a big realization.)

You eat food? My food?

VI: *(Stuffing her face:)* I'm sorry but I'm hungry and I've no time for good manners. I can pay you back, maybe, with something in the trunk.

(Opens trunk, Fluffy reacts to all the fun things in the trunk.)

Here are a bunch of old dresses that I never liked and some

silly presentation shoes that pinched my feet. Take 'em as payment for the grub. But I MUST eat ere I faint and then I needs must continue on my quest to find my brother.

MIRA: *(All she has heard is:)* Hungry? Really?

(Mira pinches Vi.)

VI: Yeouch! Hey!

(Mira pulls out her wand and starts waving it at Vi.)

Hey! Hold it kid, I'm armed!

MIRA: Fairy, fairy silly noodle, turn into a Kinda-poodle!

(Fluffy starts racing about the stage barking uncontrollably. Vi stares in horror and confusion. Mira stares at her.)

How do you feel—do you want to bark at all? Or scratch behind your ears?

VI: *(She is caught scratching behind her ear.)* Um, no…

MIRA: What if I told you you had to carry my shoes in your mouth and roll over and play dead?

VI: Well… *(Shakes off the residual magic.)* I'd say, make me!

(Mira releases Fluffy from the enchantment, Fluffy yowls and tries to hide under the table.)

MIRA: That was my first proper spell. I made it up when I was three. I wanted a puppy and… Wait. Tell me the truth, tell me, are you real? Are you? Do you need to eat and sleep, and piddle, and cry and have tantrums?

VI: I haven't had a tantrum since I was little.

MIRA: I have them all the time. I like them. All the fairies cower and run.

VI: Oh! Is that what that is? *(Pointing at Fluffy.)* I love fairies! The only ones I've ever seen are the ones the cat leaves by the kitchen door.

FLUFFY: *(Does not take that at all well.)*

MIRA: I'm overrun by the silly things on this wretched island. I'm ever so tired of them. I'm Mira. Oh, I'm a human. *(Sniffs Vi.)* And so are you! Human, I can tell! And so gentle and handsome...

VI: Handsome?

MIRA: How did you come to be on this island, you adorable thing?

VI: I'm afraid *I* must pass, I must find my brother...

MIRA: *(Suddenly angry:)* Go?! Ah... You must be one of those awful trolls trying to play a trick on me! I'll turn you into a horrible lumpy toad!

VI: No, Miss Mira, I'm a real human, I promise... I was on a ship...and there was a terrible wreck!

MIRA: OH! Me too!!! I wrecked on a ship too! I don't remember, tho', cause I was just a baby.

VI: My brother and I were traveling to the Outlands by ourselves, a small-ish vessel, but are good sailors. That storm wasn't like anything we'd ever seen before.

MIRA: I was rather proud of it.

VI: You?

MIRA: Fluffy dropped my favorite crystal ball to the floor and shattered it into a million shard-ses and I got so angry... The storm was an accident. But a good one. I've never called up sea monsters before! Oh... *(Catches herself.)* No, not really, just pretending. Terrible storms seem to happen on this island and no one can explain them! Heh. I'm glad you are alive. And here. With me.

VI: The boat cracked in twain, just like us. I held my brother but I lost him. A terrible-wonderful creature saved me and I think, I hope, he might have saved Bast. I have to find him!

(As Vi stands to go, Mira puts her wand behind her back and casts a little spell to keep Vi still.)

MIRA: Creature?

VI: He had horns, big ones and an odd demeanor, He was looking through my trunk and he was wet, and he was only half human…

(Fluffy perks at the information.)

MIRA: Horns? Surly, rude and mechanical? Oh! That was Cal. The rottenest, stinkiest, thievingest gargoyle in this pretty place. I'm sure he never pulled you out. He's tottery afraid of the water. It must've been the dolphins.

VI: No, he did. He was brave. I didn't know magical creatures could be kind to humans. Not after the way we treat them.

MIRA: Do not mention that creature to me again. He is very, VERY dangerous. I doubt he helped you, and even if he did, the ugly thing was probably waiting 'till you dried off so that he could eat you. You can't trust the magical.

(Mira starts casting a sleeping spell on Vi.)

VI: No! I… oh… suddenly I don't feel so well.

MIRA: Come home with me. You are cold, aren't you? So very, very cold. How odd… Your lips are turning quite an interesting shade of blue.

VI: *(Teeth chattering:)* But my brother…

(Faints on top of Fluffy, who is taken by surprise and is squashed. It chitters at Mira, scolding her.)

MIRA: Hush, Fluff! Oh joy! Now he's stopped talking he can't object to being helped! Best take him back home, I guess...

FLUFFY: *(Asks about Vi's brother.)*

MIRA: The brother? I doubt he made it out of there alive. Very few escape the sea's anger. We are lucky just to get the one darling thing... I'm sure he's wrong. It was never that awful Cal who saved him. He's too selfish. I think I'll send a darling little plague of grasshoppers to torment him tonight. Let's go home.

(Fluffy tries clumsily to pick Vi up.)

Oh for Minerva's sake! Just enchant him!

(Fluffy "enchants" Vi [The actor playing Vi should keep her eyes closed but stand], takes her by the hand, and follows Mira out.)

I wonder what his name is? *(Looks at trunk:)* East India Shipping Company! Delicious.

(Exit.)

SCENE 2

(Mira's bedroom. There are various found objects on the walls, including a sword. Mira is playing nurse, fussing over Vi and trying to make her comfortable. Fluffy is very unhelpful, messing up everything Mira is trying to accomplish.)

MIRA: Now, East, thou must sleep, and if you should have need of any other thing, Fluffy will attend on thee.

FLUFFY: *(Grumbles.)*

MIRA: *(Tweaking Fluffy by the ear.)* Don't be difficult!

VI: Mira! That must hurt her! Er...him?

MIRA: It, it's an it. Fairies are its.

FLUFFY: *(Hisses at Mira. Then flounces, owning its "It-ness.")*

MIRA: Fluffy's like a cat, nothing doesn't bother it!

VI: Mira, a cat would scratch you for hurting it, and then scamper away never to be seen again. You mustn't be unkind to living things.

MIRA: Foo, it's just a fairy.

VI: *(Cautiously petting Fluffy:)* I've never seen one ALIVE before. Or quite so big. Or so very, very pretty…

FLUFFY: *(Cooing at the attention, it starts to show off for Vi.)*

MIRA: It's sweet and all, but it can't chat with me, and when I ask it to braid my hair, it puts nixie knots in it, which take me forever to unravel. It's dreadful at pretend games, and when I'm feeling sad and want a cuddle it runs as far away as possible so I can't reach it. Impossible! Can't rely on a fairy!

(Bell tolls.)

I have to get to bed so Papa can read me a chapter of the "Lives of the Naiads"! *(Tucks VI in tighter:)* 'Night!

VI: Papa? I thought there were no other humans…

FLUFFY: *(About to spill the beans…)*

MIRA: *(Hastily:)* Come on Fluff-head. I need you to be my pillow! Goodnight sweet prince.

(Gives Vi a shy kiss. Vi is touched but confused.)

VI: Er…

(Mira exits.)

FLUFFY: *(Still flirting with Vi, it chatters away until Mira comes back and pokes her in the bottom. Indignant Fluffy exits, complaining the whole way.)*

(When the coast is clear Vi throws off her heavy blanket and gets dressed.)

VI: Laws, what a fuss over someone heading off to sleep… I never told her I was a prince! What means this girl-ling?

Fortune forbid my outside must have charmed her…

(Looks in the mirror.)

I do look just like Bastie. Handsome. Hmmph. The poor boy was always swatting away the silly girls. But Mira… Well. She acts silly, but I feel I'd be wrong to underestimate her… Just as she shouldn't be so trusting with me! Now how in the blazes do I get out so I can look for Bast?

CAL: *(Off:)* If Bast is a beast much like you then found he is!

VI: Oh! *(She grabs her sword.)* Wild thing, I know how to strike!

CAL: *(Suddenly appearing in the window:)* Puny thing, you'se no need. Altho' you'se would be better off wit something more attuned to yer tiny size. A toothpick fer instance.

VI: Scorpions are tiny, yet the wise man minds their sting!

(Vi runs at Cal. He grabs a sword off the wall and they fight.)

Mira said you wanted to eat me!

(A heated battle that Vi wins.)

CAL: Awright, Mam'selle Scorpina, I has noted. Yer exactly like all humans. Full of prejudice an' fear. You win. *(Cal goes to exit, turns.)* It's jes' that, I know you want yer Bast-beast and I reckon, I knows where to find him.

VI: You do? Tell me quickly!

CAL: *(Suddenly elegant:)* I come as friend, unarmed, re-sheath your weapon. *(Pauses.)* Yer too skinny to eat, anyways.

VI: Oh. *(Drops sword.)* How do you know where he is?

CAL: I reckon I fished two odd fishes out t' sea this day.

VI: Mira said you were frightened of water. And that you never did anything unless it was for your own good. Are you holding Bast prisoner?

CAL: *(Defensively:)* I may be a mite careful, where the ocean is concerned. The fish I fish out sometimes gives a good ache in the belly, like Missy Mira fer instance. But me Ma taught me t' swim, I can do it if I needs to. And I'm not a sorcerer given to putting people under lock and key! Bah. I know she dun' trust me, but I thought you and me understood one another.

VI: Alright then. I take you at your word. You've done more for me than Mira has. And to be honest, I think she's trying to keep me for a pet!

CAL: Well 'en lets be off a'fore she comes back and tries to marry ye. *(Sighs.)* Ah for a pretty face like your'n. Mayhaps she'd look at me with fondness once in a while. Bah. Throw on warmer togs, it's cold and your pelt is thin.

VI: *(Grabbing a cloak:)* I'm ready.

(Cal leaps out the window. From the whooshing sound it is obviously a long drop, Vi is alarmed.)

CAL: *(Off. Calling up:)* Jump, I'll catch ye.

VI: *(Looking down:)* Gaws. I survived a shipwreck…only to die in a leap of faith.

(She jumps, we hear a soft whump. Cal has caught her.)

VI: *(Off:)* Lead the way, wild one!

SCENE 3

(Cal and Vi in a forest, all around them lights twinkle and buzz. Cal occasionally swats at a light which then scolds him. The lights are fairies. [Again could be Fluffy with a flashlight.])

CAL: Git off me ear then, ya knave, it tickles right fierce! Keep the lights ahead so we can see!

VI: What is that?

CAL: Princess Haughty-Snot Miranda calls it Mab. Ye puny humans can't pronounce true fairy names.

VI: *(Catching and cupping Mab in her hands:)* Mab? Oh she's so tiny! Like an agate stone! So cute…OW…!!!

CAL: Watch ems, they bite when insulted. Mabby there is royalty and apt to get a wee bit agitato.

VI: How can something so pretty be so painful?

CAL: They'se just protectin' themselves. They has magic an all, but they'se don't know how to keep it, they gamble it away, or lose it in the dandelions. The foolish things let that haughty-snot Mira have too much power over 'em a'cause she's pretty! Bah. They'se fools for pretty things. *(Slyly:)* P'raps that's why they let YOU be. *(Vi looks indignant.)* Look M'Lady, don't ye be fooled by her childishness. She's a bundle of power under the candy surface, Missy Miranda is. A witch-let. And that idiot Fluffy lets her get away with too much, 'cause Mira let Fluffy out of an oak tree. *(He stops suddenly.)* 'Ere. I left the beastie restin' 'ere.

(They are in an enchanted glen.)

(Gently:) Look little one. I was able to pull you out 'afore the water got too deep in your soul. Your brother, tho', was so far gone I almost couldn't find the spark of light in him at all. The body-shell is in a state, dunno if it will live.

VI: The body-shell? What mean you?

CAL: He's empty. Not dead, but not quite alive either. The soul can't fly too far from the body. But I can't find it. Must be somewhere at the bottom of the sea.

(BAST is on the ground hidden in some leaves. He looks just like Vi. He also looks dead. Vi cries out and runs to him. She puts an ear to his chest. Hears nothing.)

VI: This is my fault, my fault! I convinced him to run away with me! I was trying to keep him alive and I've killed him. *(She takes her sword out.)* I'm going to join you, Bastie.

CAL: Stop that!!

(He tackles Vi, she fights back, remarkably strong for a girl her size. The fairy lights surround her. She calms down.)

Ow. That were a fair clout! Why do you humans value your own lives so little? I tol' ya, he's not dead! There are still things that can be done!

VI: I was with my mother when she breathed her last. She charged me with caring for Bast. And I've done nothing but muck it up. What can we do?

CAL: *(Uneasy:)* We COULD take him to Missy Mira, I s'pose. She's got the skill of healing... But... Me mother was a sorceress, I'll find out a way to keep him here, there must be somethin' in one of the books!

VI: *(Arms around Bast:)* We've no time to search through books! Please Cal, help me carry him to Mira. If she can really help him, she must! And you have been so kind to him... Please help me!

CAL: But lady, if we takes him to her, ye'll both be bound prisoners!

MIRA: *(Off:)* Gather, you fairies!

(A dreadful roar of thunder and flash of lightning. Enter Mira and Fluffy. In an instant an army of zooming flashing lights coalesce around Mira. This is her fairy army. Fluffy looks uneasy.)

Dreadful Cal-i whom I've banned! Remove thy cursed hooves from off my new-found friend or by my awesome skill thy bones shall ache anon!

CAL: *(Snarling:)* She ain'ts just yer friend. She's a brave knightess and can chooses her own way!

MIRA: She!

VI: Mistress, I tried to tell you, but you enchanted me before I could reveal the truth.

MIRA: *(Wielding her wand in a threatening manner:)* Silence, false one! I warned thee, Cal. Your ugly insides match your ugly outside. You must needs stop your interfering ways or the only thing left of you will be your rotten name. There's a lovely old oak just itching for a new prisoner! Thief and liar!

CAL: I didn't lie! I bent the truth a bit, for your sake! I wanted you not to be a'feared!

(Mira strikes with her wand as Cal approaches. He writhes in pain as does Bast.)

VI: Twin!

CAL: When we were babes together you didn't mind. I put my head in your lap and you would comb the nits out of my hair. You cared for me when my mother passed. We cared for each other.

MIRA: You took something from me. I am in pain, Cal—give me back the flower that you stole.

CAL: That flower muddles your senses, and dims your light. 'Tis time for you to face reality.

MIRA: It makes life on this island bearable! Give it back!

VI: Stop! You're hurting Bast!

MIRA: Give it back or you join your evil mother!

CAL: Don't you talk bad about me mum!

(Cal rushes Mira as she angrily raises her wand, Cal is hit with a painful bolt of magic and so is Bast. Bast's body spasms then lies still. Fluffy goes to him, working to keep him alive.)

VI: *(Frantic:)* Stop, Mira! Leave Cal alone! He rescued me and my twin from certain death. He is a brave creature!

MIRA: Cal is no great hero. My father and I were wrecked upon this isle, his wicked mother was the cause.

CAL: Lies! 'Twas betrayal from your OWN kind! And your father's lack of skill…

MIRA: The ship broke into a million pieces. My father magicked me to land.

CAL: Me mum 'twas the one who kept yer leaky basket afloat! She saved you, and went back for your father. She drowned! And then—

MIRA: Don't say anything further! Give me the flower. Give it to me—I can't bear the pain!

CAL: You're too old to hide from the truth, Missy Mira!

(Mira uses her wand to strikes a hard blow at Cal.)

MIRA: It hurts too much!!

VI: Stop it, Stop it!… Bast!

(Bast's body gives a huge shudder and stops moving.)

(Moaning in pain:) Baaaast! Sebastian! Fluffy, is he there?

FLUFFY: *(No.)*

VI: Where is he? I can't feel him. From the moment we split in our mother's belly we always knew the other's pain and happiness. Now. Blackness! OH! CAL! Mira! Please, please!!!

CAL: *(Staggers from the pain:)* Missy. Her halfling is in trouble, near death…

MIRA: DON'T SAY THAT WORD!!!

CAL: Near gone, then…probably close to all gone… I grabbed him, but felt a pull from th' god of the seas. He got the boy's soul. Quit messin' with me, I'll leave ya forever, I'll move to the biggest hill, dig a hole an' never leave, but us n' our fightin' shouldn't leave the Lady Vi bereft.

VI: *(Desperate:)* Please Mira, please. Cal says you can heal things…

MIRA: *(Changing, softening:)* Oh laws, lady! Kittens, fairies, maybe once I helped a lame unicorn. I'm just a little girl. I can't…REALLY help anyone…

CAL: Once you put me back together after a fearsome beating by them trolls—

MIRA: Shut it. Don't speak to me. *(Moving to Bast.)* Oh dear, he's barely a flutter. *(Looks from Bast to Vi.)* And as lovely as you.

(She places her hand on Bast's heart.)

Barely a sigh. Barely a whisper. But…his soul is in the ocean. It is still whole. There is hope yet. Brother octopus may have stolen his soul. Octopi love pretty things. Yes…

(She sparks a light from her wand into her hand. Bast's body goes rigid. The wind howls, the sky darkens and an unearthly glow envelops Bast and Mira.)

VI: Mira! *(Praying:)* Oh, lord of the deep!

(Mira is in a trance, the storm becomes almost unbearable. Suddenly she seems much older.)

MIRA: Great business must be wrought in time. Among the shells, inside the brine, there floats a rap'trous soul profound; I'll find it, make it come to ground.

(All of a sudden everything freezes. Only Mira moves.)

Where has Neptune hidden your soul? *(With power:)* Give me his soul, Great God of the Sea. I, Miranda, Prospero's heir, command it!

Ta-na-shen, Ca-na -fe-raciio Te Hah Bast!

(A loud noise. Mira raises her arms, and then, as if being struck in the middle of her body, she falls. Mira stands, holding a sea shell, opens it and removes a pearl.)

Here it is!

(Mira puts the pearl in Bast's mouth. His body relaxes into a natural sleep. On that, Mira also relaxes, and the storm stops. Mira goes back to being a young, scared and angry little girl. She collapses, spent.)

CAL: *(Astonished:)* Laws of heaven, hell and cosmology!

VI: He's well! I can feel him with me. Oh he's breathing well! Bast, my dear one! *(Overwhelmed:)* Oh Mira, that was… *(Words fail her.)*

CAL: *(Enthusiastically:)* Missy! Yer a more powerful witch than me mum was, than yer pa was, than Hecate herself maybe!!! You have a talent, a skill, laws, to control the sea…!

MIRA: I am NOT a witch. Don't you ever lie about that again. I just— You said you were going forever. So go. Darken not my threshold… I NEVER wish to see your face anon!

CAL: *(Stunned:)* You've no right, after what we've been through, you an' me. After the things we've meant to each other?

MIRA: Save the useless words… Go.

CAL: Right. I'm off then. *(To Vi:)* Sorry, my Lady-boy.

(Cal runs out. Bast sighs, looks up, sees Mira and:)

BAST: You… I thought you were a naiad, a narwhal, or a mermaid! Oh brave new world…

(Bast faints.)

MIRA: *(To Vi:)* Miss-behaver. You, I'm locking up in the tower. Him, *(Indicates Bast:)* I'm keeping.

(Lights out.)

SCENE 4

(Mira and Bast are having tea, as in the scene with Vi and Mira earlier. Bast is stuffing his face. Mira is clearly exhausted.)

MIRA: Are you done yet, sweeting? We have been at this table a loooong, long time…

BAST: I'll have another of the fried quail and perhaps another piece of pickled basilisk…

MIRA: At once.

(She points her wand at the table and Fluffy appears carrying a dish. Fluffy is exhausted too.)

BAST: So delicious! What on earth is taking Vi so long, she ought to have been eating long ere now?

FLUFFY: (*Tells Bast that Mira has imprisoned her.*)

(Mira interrupts.)

MIRA: She's fine. She…needs her rest, finding you so very dead tired her out! And speaking of which, aren't YOU tired of eating yet?

BAST: I feel like I haven't eaten for a week of years.

MIRA: Well hurry up!… Uh…sweeting. The music will start soon, and then we can have a dance

(Fluffy flutters flirtatiously at him. Starts playing a crazy tune, perhaps on a kazoo.)

BAST: Dance, eh? Well, I'll beg off. Not much of a dancer. More of a scientist, you know. In fact, I'd love to know how you harness the power to make your magic! I mean I've had pedagogues who can do minor stuff. Disappearing coins and such. Impressive to the peasants but nothing at all to what you can do. How'd you learn? Books?

MIRA: No not books.

BAST: Well, how then?

MIRA: Can't we just dance a little bit?

(Fluffy starts playing louder and dancing.)

BAST: Only if you want your toes trod on. *(Back to his question:)* My old tutor, Holofernes, would be very interested to know the incantation you used to revive me. It sounded Assyrian or Babylonian, can't tell which I'm afraid, as my ancient languages are a bit rusty and my accent is quite middle earth. A powerful witch like you—

MIRA: Don't call me that. Please.

BAST: *(Kindly:)* Lady Mira, I don't have the fear of magic that infects my peers, and I'm not trying to be rude, but clearly you are a...well...you use magic better than anyone I've ever seen. What does that make you?

MIRA: *(Tears in her eyes.)* Different. It makes me different.

BAST: Pooh. No sense weeping. Vi and I are both "different." Never could keep her in skirts, she likes to fight and run and play with the fellas. Me, well, I like to stay indoors and mess about with my astrolabe.

MIRA: But I will never be accepted by the world of humans. That's what Cal said. He said humans don't want a...a...witch. That humans don't trust those who are different. That I could be killed or worse if I left the island, and my pa—

BAST: Where is this pa of yours, Mira? I'd like to meet him.

MIRA: He's too busy to meet with you. He spends all of his time locked in his room trying to learn enough magic to get revenge on the people who banished him.

BAST: Revenge?

MIRA: Revenge, on the people who put us in a boat to die at sea. Because they feared us.

BAST: We've always been taught that the magical are dangerous.

MIRA: They aren't!

BAST: We are fools to fear blindly those we do not know.

MIRA: I'm so lonely on this island. No one to play with since we banished Cal.

BAST: Then un-banish him. Cal may be a queer looking sort, but there's a good egg underneath.

MIRA: I don't know... You can be my friend.

BAST: Me and Vi, you mean.

MIRA: She tried to trick me too. She didn't trust me enough to tell me the truth.

BAST: Well as to that, you don't tell the truth either. Denying who you really are is a big lie. Being a witch—

MIRA: I am NOT a WITCH. *(Trying to stay calm:)* Let's just dance.

(She makes Bast stand with her wand.)

BAST: All right then. Where are the musicians?

(Fluffy is offended.)

MIRA: I'll just conjure them...

BAST: No normal girl conjures musicians, or orders fairies around, or can call up the power of the sea! Face up to the truth of you Lady, you ARE a witch.

MIRA: *(She loses her temper:)* God's BELLS! Don't be such an ASS!

(Bast freezes. Lights and sound as he grows a pair of donkey ears. [Fluffy fixes an ass's knoll on Bast's head. Fluffy also throws fairy glitter on him.] Bast feels his ears.)

BAST: *(Delighted.)* Oh, I say!!! This is fun!!! Good bye mistress!

(He quickly trots around Mira and then leaps out the window away.)

MIRA: No, No! Come back here! Where are you going? Please, I...I didn't mean... Oh please... *(Frustrated:)* Why does no one stay?

(Fluffy shrugs.)

SCENE 5

(Vi's cell. Vi is pacing rapidly. Mira enters with Fluffy close behind. Fluffy hides.)

MIRA: YOU! You and your wicked twin...why did you have wash up on my island? To plague me?

VI: Lady, I was trying to save my brother!

MIRA: Your life must be awful for you to run away.

VI: Our da raised us alone after Ma died. He's a soldier. He blames himself for me being so boyish. And he doesn't understand Bast at all.

MIRA: I don't understand humans. At all.

VI: I want to fight with the soldiers, but girls ain't allowed. Bast wants to study, but we haven't the money. We had a nasty row, my da and me. He told me to mind my place, "You're nothing but a girl! Keep your nose out of things you don't understand!" I was so angry.

MIRA: I bet he's sad you're gone.

VI: I doubt it.

MIRA: I wish there was someone waiting back home for me.

VI: M'Lady, I know I'm not much older and therefore have no right to offer aid, but why not let Cal be your friend? He speaks rough, but inside he's kinder than most.

MIRA: Cal hates me.

VI: I thought you hated him?

MIRA: I tried to make him be less ugly, I tried to make him more "normal," and he only laughed and *(In Cal's voice:)* "owned I didn't mind how I looked." I've been really cruel to him, and he lets me. He's been father and brother to me.

VI: Brothers can be a real pain, M'Lady.

MIRA: *(Tortured:)* Oh Vi. When I was a tiny baby, I cried, and I would destroy everything around me. I couldn't control my magic. My nursemaid was frightened of me, and told the townspeople that I was a witch and I was to be *(Can't say killed:)*...destroyed. My father and I escaped on a ship, but I was so little and so hungry, I cried and screamed, and the sea responded. I caused such a storm. Such a storm. Such a wreck.

When I awoke to life, my father was by my side, as was Cal. Cal became my playmate and companion. My brother and beloved.

But, in truth Cal was giving me a potion. A potion that muddled my senses, and kept me happy and babyish. And, now that I'm older, he has been keeping the potion from me, and my eyes have been opened to my own truth, and my wickedness. My father...my father drowned. And Cal's mother died trying to save him.

VI: *(Kindly:)* Lady. Perhaps his deceptions were meant to cushion you from a hard truth. Lying is unforgivable, I know, but sometimes it's done to keep a heart from breaking.

MIRA: He knows I can't control my craft. And I can't. I am dangerous and I am becoming deluded and muddleheaded.

VI: Maybe you can come home with me and Bast.

MIRA: Bast! Oh!... He's... He's... Oh I did it again...

VI: What?!

MIRA: I'm sorry, Vi. You need to stay here until I can sort things out for myself. I'm sorry.

(She puts a locking hex on the door and exits.)

VI: Oh Fluffy, what am I to do? That silly Bast has got himself in trouble again. I have to make things right! We've got to figure a way out of this room!

FLUFFY: (*Fluffy indicates in mime that it knows a way to circumvent Mira's curse.)*

VI: You can help me out of here? How?

FLUFFY: (*Tries to convey in fairy language and mime that what she needs to do is fly.*)

VI: Fluffy, Fluffy, I can't understand a thing, slow down!

FLUFFY: *(Yes you can, it's quite simple. [A long pantomime on the correct way to take flight.])*

VI: What in the name of...

FLUFFY: *(Very frustrated, maybe louder.)*

VI: For Minerva's sake I don't speak fairy!!

FLUFFY: *(Slowly:)* F—l—l—l—y—y—y?

VI: Fly??

FLUFFY: *(YES. In triumph!)*

VI: But Fluffy, how am I supposed to fly? Will you shower me in pixie dust?

FLUFFY: *(Looks scornfully at Vi as if that is the silliest thing it's ever heard. Does another pantomime on the correct way to fly.)*

VI: Oh Fluffy, I can't do that! That takes brains and skill...

FLUFFY: *(And trusting that someone else knows better than you do.)*

VI: Alright. I trust you, Fluffy. I can't stay trapped and neither can you, no matter how much I'd like to help Mira.

(Fluffy begins a slow dance. Vi starts to dance with it and looks curiously at Fluffy to see what to do next. Fluffy grabs Vi's hand and jumps out the window, Vi leaps, we hear the same drop, a yelp, a swoosh, then the sound of flight and a delighted yell from Vi. Mira runs into the room.)

MIRA: I am betray'd!

SCENE 6

(Cal's camp. Bast's donkey ears have gotten much bigger. Cal is leafing through a huge spell-book. The fairy lights are buzzing and chirping at him.)

CAL: Hamster Livers, Hens' Teeth, Hexes, Removal... Laws, Mum, why didn't ya bother ta write a bit larger...? Is that Yew or Pew, Mabby? Bah, I need a rolling pin, a bucket of soap suds and a cheerful dwarf for this one. T'll never work. I've never met anyone more surly than a dwarf. Bother, bother, bother!

BAST: *(Cheerfully:)* No worries, Cal old snoot. I'm utterly delighted to be one of you! Hee-haw!!

(He starts to skitter away, Cal grabs him.)

CAL: Yer not going anywhere!! Blast, where's your sister?!

Mira must've locked her up but good.

BAST: Vi-vi will find her way out. She's resourceful, that one. There's not an Abbess in all of Blighty that was able to keep Vi at her prayers; she was a regular escape artist. Could fit through the smallest crack in any wall. Helped that she's so low and little. Da would send her off to school and she'd ditch the nurse and end up back home before you could say "'Twas the winter of our discontent." She'll be here soon.

CAL: She better, yer almost done for! If we don't get the curse off you, you'll be stuck as a fairy for'e'r and no remedy for it.

BAST: There are worse fates, I suppose. I like being a magical creature! No one to demand I sword fight them, hee-haw! If confronted I can simply fly away! Rawther a good fate I should think!

CAL: I keeps tellin' ye, ye pure human types, if you are left magicked too long, you go feral and wild and try to take over the fairy kingdom and then the queen and king have you for tea… Yer too old ta be a changeling…

VI: *(Whooping from off:)* Oh bother!!…

(Loud crash as Vi hurtles herself into Cal's Lair. Fluffy arrives a few seconds later and stops comfortably.)

BAST: *(Picking Vi up and dusting her off:)* VI! I knew you would figure a way out!

VI: *(Hugging him:)* Cheeky monkey! Thought for sure I'd lost you and here you are, obnoxious as always. OH!

CAL: Cautions there, Bast has been…translated.

(Vi takes in the donkey ears, Bast brays with joy.)

VI: O Bastie, thou art changed! What do I see on thee?!

(He cocks his head to look at her.)

BAST: You are a sight of delight, dearest twinnie-twinsie. Tho' I knew you'd escape to the forest, I thought maybe Mira had turned you into a ferret or a newt or something like that. Say, what do you think of my new saucers?

VI: Dear one, you look very silly! *(Points to ears.)* Take 'em off, I don't like them. I don't like it when you playact.

BAST: Says her worship, the girl in boy's garb.

VI: *(Defensively:)* It's COMFORTABLE.

BAST: Da hates it!

VI: Da's not here. Take off those stupid ears!

BAST: Make me!

VI: I will!

(They start to tussle. It takes Cal a bit to pry them apart.)

CAL: Did the two of you split the one brain in half then? Settle down. *(Indicating ears:)* He can't take the blasted things off any more'n I can.

BAST: Nor don't want to, neither, old bean.

VI: Why? Bast, they're awful…

BAST: No, no, no! Aesthetically beautiful they may not be, but I hear better, and if I concentrate hard enough I can fly, watch!

(He makes a wind up motion and the ears propel him clumsily into the air [He jumps high], it is graceless, but he is delighted.)

VI: Stop it! Bast, stop it at once!

(Bast ignores her.)

BAST: I feel wonderful! These ears, silly as they seem, make things CLEAR. I can hear cowslips sway, and I can see so far that I can make out the pattern in a bumblebees eye!

CAL: 'Tis 'cause you are made of fairy-stuff. Ye have the hearing and sight of a magic being.

FLUFFY: *(Hello. Frostily. It proceeds to scold Cal in physical mime.)*

CAL: C'mon, I never meant for ye t' be trapped in that minx's lair so long. Say, as thanks for bringin' the twinnie-twinsies together, I'll give ye back yer little bit of magic that I stole. I kept it all this while.

(Cal removes a small flower from a locket around his neck, he gives it to Fluffy, who jumps around joyously. It takes a deep smell and places it in its ear. It hugs Cal.)

I only meant to play a trick on ye, a'cause you were acting such a fool. Now yer in the forest to stay and Missy ain't got no power over you as your magic is complete.

VI: Fluffy, Cal, what about Bast's magic? How do we get him back together?

BAST: *(Uncooperative:)* Don't want that silly heavy body, Vi-la. I'm free now, I fly! I can taste stars! I am LIGHT! No one's going to catch me now and steal my stamps and treasures!

CAL: I bin' searchin', best as I kin make out we need to coax him to heave off the fairy stuff on his own and will himself back human. Then we say the incantation all at th' same time, and he should be put back. His essential humanity is like a sea-sponge, if he 'lows he want's t' be whole, he will be, but the fool keeps natterin' on about wantin' to stay!

BAST: Well, I do want to stay. I'm here now, I like the form, I was never all that happy as a clumsy hulking fellow anyhow.

CAL: So ye want to forget yer human life!?

FLUFFY: *(Being a fairy is not all it's cracked up to be!)*

VI: You dope, I'm not a magic being! That makes us untwinned. D'ya want to cast me off thus? And how can I get off this island and make my way back home without you?

BAST: Silly Vi, you're the one who took me away from home in the first place! Say hello to… Oh what is his name? The man who cares for us?

VI: Da, Bast. Our da! Our father!

BAST: Da… You mean Daddy. We used to call him Daddy, didn't we, before we got so grown up?

VI: Yes, Bast. And Daddy'll be ever so sad if you don't come home. Who will teach him what the shapes in the rocks mean, or show me a dragon's bone or make us both laugh when we are fighting with each other? C'mon. Let's go back home.

BAST: *(A difficult decision:)* Promise me that there will be no more running away. We will tell Da exactly how we feel and ask him to accept us in our own skins, as our own true selves. To our own selves we'll be true.

(They embrace.)

VI: Yes, Bastie! No more hiding our true natures.

BAST: Yes, then. Yes. If I can live as myself, I've no need to be enchanted.

CAL: Well done, twinnies! Come 'ere, Fluff,

(Cal shows them a bit of text in the book)

we must say it together and you must drop a drop of your flower into his mouth.

FLUFFY, VI & CAL: *(Fluffy in its language:)* Take this transformed scalp from off the head of this Sebastian; that, he awaking may think no more of this night's accidents but as the fierce vexation of a dream.

(Bast glows, then a huge sound, and he is a normal boy, no ears, no fairy glitter and slightly myopic. He shakes himself like a

dog.)

BAST: *(Sheepish:)* It IS a bit like waking up from a dream. I'm sorry to have woken up, but everything does look better in the light of reality.

VI: Here are your glasses, dearest Twinnie-twinsie.

CAL: Look-ses, Gemini, I has liked havin' yer around and all, and I HATE to be nice, BUT. We've gots to get you off this isle and back home.

VI: *(Guiltily:)* I do reckon our departure has caused quite the uproar. Poor Da… How do we get off this island and back?

CAL: Well…I…I has made a ship.

BAST, VI & FLUFFY: You did!?

CAL: Yeah'rr, I put it together from the bibs and bobs of the vessels that wash up on this isle with alarmin' frequency. I reckon it'll make it to th' Outlands, with good luck and good weather, if yer willin' to try it. I was makin' it for HER.

BAST: But Cal, and *(Indicating Fluffy:)* you too, little fairy, you must come with us! We are boon friends now and will find you places at court, and you need never be abused or unloved again.

FLUFFY: *(Buzzing unhappily, it dances about how it would never leave Mira.)*

CAL: It's a fine idea, an' I'm tempted, knowin' you two and bein' curious an all about the wide world, but…Fluffy and I, we are all Mira's got, her pa being long dead… He died in the original shipwreck as a matter o' fact, and between her fear and her grief she very nearly died as well. WE make her illusions, me an' Fluff an' the other fairy-folk, we create her pa out of star-stuff every day and he appears to her and he loves her, and one day, when Fluffy and I get cleverer, we will gently wreck another ship and get 'em to take her home wif' 'em.

VI: Oh Cal…we COULD take Mira with us. She needs to be with humans like herself. Help us convince her to come.

CAL: *(Reluctantly:)* But then I'd be left without her, and I can't bear that jus' yet. Let Mira keep her illusions. Let me keep mine. And anyhow, she hasn't got control over her gifts of magic yet. If she's let out into the real world and loses her temper, she might be banish-ed like me mum. Or worse. Witches are burnt in the Outlands.

VI: There are people in the Outland too ignorant to ask questions before they start the fire. But, Cal, the LEAST we could do is reconcile you with her… Before we go, there MUST be a way…

BAST: I say… I think I have an idea…as long as that ship of yours IS sail-able… Have you any spells in that book that can conjure costumes?

SCENE 7

(The beach. Mira is playing sadly alone. She is idly making strands of seaweed dance.)

MIRA: Where the fox cries there cry I; In a tulip's shell I lie;
There I couch when robins fly.
On the summers breeze I sigh
After winter merrily.
Merrily, merrily shall I live now
Under the blossom that hangs on the bough.

(Fluffy enters panicked. A pantomime about Cal being in trouble. Suddenly we hear Cal shouting.)

CAL: *(Off:)* Help me! Oh help me, Missy Mira!

*(Fluffy and Mira run to look. They watch the audience as if it

was the sea.)

MIRA: Fluffy! It's not another ship?! What is that, in the distance? A sea monster?

FLUFFY: (*Mimes that it does indeed look like a sea monster.*)

MIRA: That silly fool Cal what is he doing?? Look Fluff! The monster comes closer!… *(Screams in fear.)* Ah! Cal, watch out! It's right behind you!! There's another one!

(Fluffy is practically wiggling out of its wings in effort. It is miming a heated battle.)

Go Fluffy, you must help Cal!

(Fluffy puts a toe in the water and flatly refuses to go in.)

CAL': *(Off:)* Help me. *(Louder and more insistently:)* Ahem! Help me!!!

(Fluffy finally gets pushed by Mira to get into the water. It runs into the audience.)

MONSTER (VI): *(Off:)* You're finally mine you big, juicy, delicious beastie!!

SECOND MONSTER (BAST): *(Off:)* Not if I get him first! Yum Yum!

(The monsters roar fiercely, sounds of a battle as Mira watches. [Vi, Bast, Fluffy, and Cal could be in the audience. Bast and Vi dressed as a sea serpent or a Megalodon.])

MIRA: No, he is MY dearest friend, you shan't hurt him!!!!

(Mira begins to chant.)

Let them be hunted soundly. At this hour lie at my mercy all mine enemies: Shortly shall all my labours end, and thou shalt have the air at freedom.

(She calls up a huge storm. There is a lot of noise, wind, thunder. We hear Cal and Fluffy panicking, then:)

BAST & VI: *(Ad lib sounds of distress.)* Nooo, help!!!

MIRA: Blow, winds and crack your cheeks! Rage! Blow!

CAL: *(Off:)* Missy Mira! Please, I'm alright, stop the storm, yer killin' 'em!

(Fluffy runs onstage, begging Mira to stop.)

(Cal enters sputtering and wet, dragging on Bast and Vi still in costume.)

CAL: It's only the twins!

(Mira is still in a rage. She seems to have gone mad.)

MIRA: Rumble thy bellyful! Spit, fire! Spout, rain!

CAL: *(Trying to stand upright in the howling of the wind:)* Missy mine. Call off your sheets of fire, your horrid thunder! *(Begging:)* See reason! Mira! See reason!! You'll kill us all!

(Mira slowly comes back to herself, and takes in her friend's fright. She calms the storm, which seems to swirl into her. A beat as the quiet returns. In the calm she stares ruefully at Cal.)

MIRA: Oh Cal, it is so much, so much power. I wanted to cause great hurt, and the power is at my fingertips. How, HOW can I live among my people, when I am fatal to them?

VI: We have been fools, Mira. Bast and I thought we'd teach you to value your friendship with the wild-ings. Cal and Fluffy. We didn't mean to frighten you so!

BAST: Darned impressive, your gifts, however.

VI: Please, forgive us. Bast and I are ready to go home. We did not want to leave without resolving your quarrel.

MIRA: The quarrel is with myself alone. *(Desperately, weeping:)* Alone, Alone. Alone.

CAL: *(Gently:)* Missy, yer not alone. Fluff and I will take care of you, we always have…

MIRA: But you aren't LIKE me. I want to be with those like ME. I'm tired of magic. I want to be ordinary, to sleep in an ordinary bed, with an ordinary family. And to be able to be angry, without hurting someone!

CAL: *(Slightly indignant:)* You mayn't be ordinary, but neither do we want ye to be. And Fluff and I, we're yer family. We LIKE you. *(Fluffy kicks him.)* Blast it! Loves you then, you minx.

FLUFFY: *(I love you too.)*

BAST: Cal, you're a good chap. Brave and true. A trifle raw in your manners and ways, but a valiant companion.

VI: And Fluffy is clever, quick and funny, and dear.

BAST: I think the three of you make a fine family indeed.

MIRA: Three, only? But WHY must you go?

VI: We have family too.

BAST: Who are expecting us and have mourned our departure.

VI: Come with us, all of you!

MIRA: I must stay until I learn to control my powers. And until I am ready to say a permanent goodbye to my father.

CAL: *(Startled:)* So ye DO know th' truth, Missy.

MIRA: I know, I've known, I've known for a long time that he isn't quite right. But what you have made of him, the shadow Prospero, is dear and precious to me and I'm not yet ready to leave him behind.

CAL: Then you'll stay wif me…er, us?

MIRA: I will, Cal. And I'll be less unkind, and try not to take my pique out on you anymore. Or you, dear Fluff…

FLUFFY: (*Pleased.*)

VI: A goodbye kiss for you all!

(Hugs and shoulder claps all around. Cal blushes furiously.)

BAST: And Miss Mira, if ever you do reach the Outlands, please, find me and teach me your skill. I will be a willing apprentice to your magical power.

MIRA: Give me your spectacles.

(He does. She puts an enchantment on them.)

There, now you can see the magic that is in the everyday world and you can learn how to manage it on your own, as I did.

BAST: Thank you for the wondrous gift, lady. You are as generous as you are lovely.

MIRA: Perhaps you'll wreck upon my shores again.

CAL: Set sail and away. And when you hit the land of the mud men, remember us with kindness.

(The twins exeunt.)

(Privately to Mira as they watch them leave:) Missy Mira, d'ya crave the forgettin' potion? I've kept it from you now for so long. That was cruel of me.

MIRA: No, Cal. Curse me. The truth pains me greatly, but I must needs reconcile with it.

CAL: Missy Mira. The growin' time is painful. We are children no longer.

(Fluffy chitters sadly at the sounds of a ship sailing away. A golden sunset.)

CAL & MIRA: Once I sat upon a promontory,
And heard a mermaid on a dolphin's back

Uttering such dulcet and harmonious breath
That the rude sea grew civil at her song
And certain stars shot madly from their spheres,
To hear the sea-maid's music.

MIRA: Goodbye my dears, my dears…

(A sad long pause. They are all lit by the golden sunset.)

CAL: One of these days we'll get the RIGHT ship to crash on this isle and then we could ALL go on an adventure.

MIRA: *(Smiles.)* Rude things, lead me to the bank where the wild thyme blows, I'm sleepy, and Pa will be waiting for me with another chapter in his book.

CAL: *(Winking at Fluffy:)* Yes, yer worship. *(Turns to the audience.)* If we shadows have offended…

MIRA: C'mon Cal!

CAL: Never mind. Pr'aps as ye get older ye'll find out the rest of the story. Play ON!

(End of play.)

The Author Speaks

What inspired you to write this play?
I started my career as a professional actor in TYA (Theatre for Young Audiences). I played an ant. I've also played aliens, cats and a giant thumb. I loved performing in those plays! They were the most fun you could possibly have onstage, even if they were exhausting. A group of us who acted in a lot of them used to joke about going to TY-AA meetings. Also, I fell in love with Shakespeare in high school. When my English teacher got annoyed with us, she would put in the video tape of Ian McKellan's *Acting Shakespeare* as a punishment. Ha! I was riveted. I wanted to BE Ian. I had fun putting two things I love so much into a mash-up TYA. And having been in so many of them, I tried to structure the show for maximum acting fun as well as audience fun.

Was the structure or other elements of the play influenced by any other work?
Totally! ***The Tempest, 12th Night,*** *Harry Potter,* Madeleine L'Engle. (Remember when she put Meg's father into a tree like Ariel in *A Wrinkle in Time*?) I always felt that Caliban got a bad shake. I loved him. He is a little weird, but he's a PERSON.

I also really enjoy it when writers take characters with whom we are familiar, and put them into new and different situations. There are lots of examples of this but Gregory Maguire's *Wicked* is a favorite.

Have you dealt with the same theme in other works that you have written?
The theme of feeling different and weird, yes. Learning to accept who you are and that your "strangeness" is what makes you unique. That is definitely something I write about a lot. Also this particular play is about children dealing with grief, growing up, maturing. As a matter of fact, the children in

Caliban's Island are loads more mature than most of the adult characters in my other plays.

What writers have had the most profound effect on your style?
Tom Stoppard, Shakespeare, Sarah Ruhl. Also Lou Reed, Patti Smith, David Bowie. I listen to a lot of different kinds of music when I write. I like rhythm and cadence in everyday speech. English is my second language and, even though I came to the US as a very little girl, I tend to write a bit floridly and elaborately, as if I were translating from Spanish. Also since I am Colombian, Gabriel García Márquez is a huge influence, most especially in his theory of magical realism. He believed that magic DOES exist in the everyday world and so do I.

What do you hope to achieve with this work?
I would like the play to start conversations about embracing your differences, about letting go of guilt when we cause accidental hurts, about making families out of your friends, about the pain of growing up. I have a son who is a lot like my character Bast. He doesn't like to do sports, he isn't loud, he's quite happy being by himself. I was a boisterous, bossy girl like Vi, and I often got scolded for not being lady-like. I'd like this play to help kids who don't quite fit in to see that it's alright to be "odd" and unique.

What were the biggest challenges involved in the writing of this play?
My son likes to "help." He once wrote "Help! I'm a Bug." into one of my scripts. (He loves *Calvin and Hobbes*.) I'm glad I found it before I sent it to the publisher!

Joking aside, a tough thing for me in writing this script was to find natural places for the characters to speak in iambic pentameter. The most enjoyable thing was dropping in little Shakespeare Easter-eggs.

What are the most common mistakes that occur in productions of your work?
Taking everything way too seriously! I'm flattered when I get a call from a director asking me EXACTLY what I want, but I want you to go for it. With ***Caliban's Island,*** I encourage a lot of improvisation for the character of Fluffy. I hope that everyone who plays Fluffy is completely different and individual! I am also passionate about diversity in casting—when I say any ethnicity, I mean it.

What inspired you to become a playwright?
I have been a mildly successful actress all of my life, nothing too flashy, but I always worked. Then the time came where there were no roles for me! None. I'm not THIS enough, I'm too much THIS, I'm too old, I'm too young. I'm so LATINA. I decided to write plays that I could perform myself. I wrote the play ***Silueta*** (with Chris and Tom Shelton) as a two-hander that I could do with my partner—we could take our young child on the road, I could work as an ACTOR, you know? (Don't get me started on childcare in the theatre!) ***Silueta*** is about the life and death of Cuban artist Ana Mendieta and her husband Carl Andre, who was accused and acquitted of her death. On a whim I submitted it to The Great Plains Theatre Conference and we were accepted. That started me on the road to thinking I could pursue writing, as I found I loved it, and I had so much more power in the room than a mere actor.

My mandate is to write great roles for women.

How did you research the subject?
I reread ***Twelfth Night, A Midsummer Night's Dream, King Lear,*** and ***The Tempest***. I also had the luxury of a staged reading with a group of fantastic actors. Having a really intelligent actor reading your work, questioning why their character does things, and then diving into the script with relish, is one of the best things for any playwright. I'm also

very lucky that I belong to Breath of Fire Latina Theatre Ensemble, a group of truly amazing performers, writers, and directors who are encouraging and engaged with new work.

Are there any characters modeled after real life or historical figures?
I teach tweens. I love them for their maturity one minute and their childishness the next. These characters are based on me, on my son Lionel and on a few lovely, inspiring students from South Coast Repertory's youth conservatory.

What is your writing process?
Write, write, cry, write, write, edit, edit, edit. I start with an idea, maybe one scene, one or two characters, then if it interests me I build a story. I do a lot of research. I read everything I can get my hands on about the subject on which I'm basing the play. I keep stacks of books on my desk for quick reference and I tape up all sorts of pictures for inspiration. Then I write as much as I can. When I think it's done, I cut a lot and do more writing. And it's never done, never good enough and constantly asking to be revised.

Shakespeare gave advice to the players in *Hamlet;* if you could give advice to your cast what would it be?
Use your voice, open your mouth and speak the speech! Be mindful of how you sound. Communication is a lost art. Cultivating a beautiful, clear voice is as much of an asset to an actor as a strong body. I came to this country speaking only Spanish, I had a lisp, and I was raised in San Jose, CA so I had a STRONG slacker accent. My first voice teacher, Victor Pappas, encouraged me to work on the way I sounded. I am so grateful to him. My voice is my secret weapon as a performer and a teacher.

Why was Mira born a witch?

Why Mira was born a witch isn't as important as the fact that she was "born that way." Like one of the mutant X-Men or Harry Potter, she suffers because she frightens "normal" people and tries to hide her true self. She starts to grow because she is honest and open with her friends. It's important to be true to yourself, and on the other side, to be open minded about people who are "different." Open your heart to empathy and kindness, you'll find yourself living a much happier life.

About the Author

Diana Burbano, a Colombian immigrant, is an Equity actor, a playwright and a teaching artist at South Coast Repertory (Costa Mesa, CA). Plays include ***Fabulous Monsters,*** a Festival51 winner, about women in punk rock, ***Picture Me Rollin'*** (featured at the 35th annual William Inge Festival.), ***Silueta,*** (about the Cuban artist Ana Mendieta), with Tom and Chris Shelton, and the TYA Shakespeare mash-up, ***Caliban's Island. Libertadoras, Vamping*** and ***Linda*** were written for the 365 Women a Year project and have been performed around the world. Her short play ***Rounds Per Second*** is featured in Smith and Kraus's 5-minute play anthology. She manages Sleep Till Noon Productions and the Gourmet Detective. Diana is one of the original members of the writers circle for Latino Theatre Association/Los Angeles. She is also a member of The Dramatists Guild and The Alliance of Los Angeles Playwrights.

About YouthPLAYS

YouthPLAYS (www.youthplays.com) is a publisher of award-winning professional dramatists and talented new discoveries, each with an original theatrical voice, and all dedicated to expanding the vocabulary of theatre for young actors and audiences. On our website you'll find one-act and full-length plays and musicals for teen and pre-teen (and even college) actors, as well as duets and monologues for competition. Many of our authors' works have been widely produced at high schools and middle schools, youth theatres and other TYA companies, both amateur and professional, as well as at elementary schools, camps, churches and other institutions serving young audiences and/or actors worldwide. Most are intended for performance by young people, while some are intended for adult actors performing for young audiences.

YouthPLAYS was co-founded by professional playwrights Jonathan Dorf and Ed Shockley. It began merely as an additional outlet to market their own works, which included a substantial body of award-winning published and unpublished plays and musicals. Those interested in their published plays were directed to the respective publishers' websites, and unpublished plays were made available in electronic form. But when they saw the desperate need for material for young actors and audiences—coupled with their experience that numerous quality plays for young people weren't finding a home—they made the decision to represent the work of other playwrights as well. Dozens and dozens of authors are now members of the YouthPLAYS family, with scripts available both electronically and in traditional acting editions. We continue to grow as we look for exciting and challenging plays and musicals for young actors and audiences.

About ProduceaPlay.com

Let's put up a play! Great idea! But producing a play takes time, energy and knowledge. While finding the necessary time and energy is up to you, ProduceaPlay.com is a website designed to assist you with that third element: knowledge.

Created by YouthPLAYS' co-founders, Jonathan Dorf and Ed Shockley, ProduceaPlay.com serves as a resource for producers at all levels as it addresses the many facets of production. As Dorf and Shockley speak from their years of experience (as playwrights, producers, directors and more), they are joined by a group of award-winning theatre professionals and experienced teachers from the world of academic theatre, all making their expertise available for free in the hope of helping this and future generations of producers, whether it's at the school or university level, or in community or professional theatres.

The site is organized into a series of major topics, each of which has its own page that delves into the subject in detail, offering suggestions and links for further information. For example, Publicity covers everything from Publicizing Auditions to How to Use Social Media to Posters to whether it's worth hiring a publicist. Casting details Where to Find the Actors, How to Evaluate a Resume, Callbacks and even Dealing with Problem Actors. You'll find guidance on your Production Timeline, The Theater Space, Picking a Play, Budget, Contracts, Rehearsing the Play, The Program, House Management, Backstage, and many other important subjects.

The site is constantly under construction, so visit often for the latest insights on play producing, and let it help make your play production dreams a reality.

More from YouthPLAYS

Prime by Ellen Margolis
Comedy. 80-85 minutes. 6 females, 6 males, 6 either.

Princess Dar and Prince Dion, young royals from neighboring kingdoms, are destined for each other through an arranged marriage. On the eve of the wedding, however, they decide to run away and discover their own futures. Escaping to a nearby valley, they cross paths with disoriented lovers, hot-headed party animals, desperate draft dodgers, and a number-obsessed hermit. Identities are investigated, resources stretched, and every kind of love put to the test.

Scareville by Julia Edwards
Comedy for Young Audiences with Music. 40-50 minutes. 3+ females, 2+ males (5+ gender-flexible performers possible).

Milo and Clare are afraid...of lots of things. And there's good reason when they find themselves trapped in Scareville one dark, haunted night, surrounded by six-foot spiders, zombies and Dr. Fear himself. Will they end up being eaten by Sally the Black Widow? Or will Mike the Zombie's lesson on brains teach them a thing or two about fear?

The Matsuyama Mirror by Velina Hasu Houston
Drama. 60-70 minutes. 4 females, 1 male, 3 either.

In Matsuyama, Japan in the 1600s, a world before the discovery of mirrors, young Aiko comes of age in the aftermath of her mother's death. Gifted with a “magic” mirror, she sees her image and believes that it is her mother's spirit—and when her father remarries and she begins to grow up, Aiko resists, escaping into an enchanted world where dolls come to life. As they encourage her to stay to play and frolic, will Aiko fall into the fantasy forever, or will she discover the true magic of life?

Rumors of Polar Bears by Jonathan Dorf
Dramedy. 90-100 minutes. 8-25+ females, 4-15+ males (14-40+ performers possible).

A ragtag band of teens hits the road to survive a climate induced catastrophe. As they encounter unfinished coloring books and failing paradises, a frozen-in-time former pre-kindergarten drama class, bikers determined to turn the chaos into their new world order, and a mysterious people that even the bikers won't cross, will the refugees follow Deme and chase after the rumored polar bears that she believes are the key to their survival, or will their patchwork family fall apart?

Les Examables by Don Zolidis
Comedy. 100-110 minutes. 8-28 females, 5-25 males (15-40+ performers possible).

Tired of too much standardized testing in her high school, high achiever Anna Ullman stages a protest and finds herself crowned the new principal. But ultimate power comes with its own problems (especially after death threats from the all-powerful State Board of Ed), and soon Anna descends into madness, imposing even more standardized testing. It's up to her former best friend, Lola, to bring down this new tyrant. Soon Lola is manning the barricades and singing triumphantly awesome songs in this insane satire based on the mega-musical ***Les Misérables***.

An Avalanche of Murder by Matt Buchanan
Comic Mystery. 75-85 minutes. 8-12 females, 4-7 males (13-16 performers possible).

In this affectionate spoof of old-fashioned murder mysteries, the Hopkins family is trapped in a house by a freak avalanche, and they're dropping like flies. It's up to young Mary and Anthony to figure out who's killing them off one by one—and bragging about it on a dead phone—before there's nobody left.

Made in the USA
San Bernardino, CA
05 June 2020